He Puts on His Poker Face

Poems by

Sharon Waller Knutson

ISBN: 978-93-6354-839-8

First Edition: 2024
Rs. 200/-

Cyberwit.net
HIG 45 Kaushambi Kunj, Kalindipuram
Allahabad - 211011 (U.P.) India
http://www.cyberwit.net
Tel: +(91) 9415091004
E-mail: info@cyberwit.net

Printed at Repro India Limited.

For Al

Acknowledgements

Lothlorien: "His Chips Come with Cod," "Kenny Rogers Sings the Gambler," "I Am Waiting For My Sweet and Sour Shrimp," "Sights You'll Never See Again," and """The Eagles Soar Inside and Out."

Red Eft Review: "A Chicken Strays from the Neighbor's Flock." "Father Knows Best," "With Six Grandsons Behind the Wheel,"

Storyteller Poetry Review: "Brother Poets," "Catfish Messages Me on Facebook," "Corresponding with Barbara Crooker," "Dancing with a Scorpion," "Even If," "Happy Birthday Sharon, She Sings," "I Am Not a Bouvier," In a Billings Bar March 6, 1963," "If Hemmingway Wrote our Love Story," 'In Our Senior Years," "I Schedule a Zoom Poetry Reading on Super Bowl Sunday," 'Guess Who is Squatting in our Sun Room," "On Netflix We watch Walt," "Pushing Eighty-Six From Peru," "Sister Poets," "She is a Rambler," "Sugar High," "The Day My Mother Takes on Terrorists," "The Muse Speaks," "The Wailing Woman." "There we are on YouTube," "The Poet at Ninety," "Trading Trains for Tarantulas" and "Walking on Air."

Your Daily Poem: "Idaho Falls 1995."

Worksheets: "The Muse Rides a Harley."

Contents

Early Life with Al

He Puts on His Poker Face

because he is the King
and I am the Queen
and we have a Full House.

Our Four of a Kind -
a daughter and three
sons – wade knee deep

in snow and watch
our Three of a Kind
grandsons - all born

a few months apart -
race their snowmobiles
like they used to while

our Five of a Kind
great grandchildren
sculpt a snowman.

Despite the cards
we are dealt –
divorce and death –

we as a family
will continue to multiply
and win the Jackpot.

Even If

The Bengals beat the Bulldogs
thanks to your ability to steal
a football and run like lightening,
I wouldn't have been there
to watch because I was home
writing my advice column
for the high school newspaper
or babysitting for college money.

Even if we had sat side by side
at the Country Bear Jamboree
at Disneyland or stood in the same
line for the Calico Log Ride
at Knott's Berry Farm
you were focused\on your family
and I was busy taking notes
for my newspaper story.

Even if while on vacation
visiting a college roommate
in Idaho I had seen
you at the barn saddling
a horse with her husband
I wouldn't have noticed
because I was married
to the newspaper business
and eager to get back
to California.

It was only when I left
my life in California
and you lost your wife
and walked into my store
looking for a book to read
and a dinner companion
that we saw each other
for the first time
and were ready for romance.

Idaho Falls Idaho – 1995

The ink barely dry on his divorce papers,
the farmer turned real estate broker
walks in the bookstore and tells me
he reads a book a day and wants to swap.
Then asks me for supper at a small café
across the river where we enjoy lobster
and baked potatoes and conversation
as smooth as the caffeine we sip until
we see the closed sign in the window
and the waitresses napping in their chairs.
Silver anniversary? the waitress asks
as he pays the check. *First date,* he says.
I nod and she laughs. *Such jokers.*

Like teenagers, we are eating corn
on the cob and shish kabob
in the bleachers at the Blackfoot Fair
as Tim McGraw sings, *I like it, I love it*
I want some more of it and we drive
in his white Buick to the top of the hill
above the tiny toy city on the tracks.
You kids go home to your folks, says
the policeman with the shiny flashlight.
I go home to my mother with melanoma
and he to his seventeen-year-old son.

Twenty-seven years later, mother long
gone, son with kids and wife of his own,
we eat grilled chicken and green beans

in Applebee's sitting smack dab in the spot
where the comfortable café once cuddled
the riverbank, but we skip the freeway
ride to the fair and pick up a DVD
by Sheryl Crow and relax in the recliner
in front of the DVD player and listen
to her sing, *Every Day is a Winding Road*
and pretend we are seeing her in person
as we revel in the landmarks of our life.

Floating on Air

in a hot air balloon
in a sky blue as the ocean
over the city of Reno
was not what I had in mind
when you proposed
but here we are in the Kodak
photos saying our vows
in red sweatshirts and blue jeans,
your hair still dark, mine
still blonde and curly,
as the rainbow colored
balloon floats without even
a soft breeze to nudge it,
and we watch people, cars
trees and houses shrink
into toys in a universe
where dreams come true.
Even in my eighties
as I fear I'll fall if I stand
on a chair or a ladder, I know
if you propose we renew
our vows, I'll book the closest
balloon and float over Phoenix
and feel like I am in heaven.

If Hemingway Wrote our Love Story

The sun would also rise
over the Superstitions
and the bulls would run
across the Arizona desert,
not Pamplona, Spain,

and you would be healthy
as your horses and I would
have flings with cowboys
long before we meet
under a full moon.

Sipping Folgers,
instead of Pernod,
we would stand,
watching through
the kitchen window

as two bulls charge
each other and lock
horns and push each
other around
in a cloud of dust

until they limp off
down the road
and we go back
to our business
of living and loving.

To My Valentine

I loved the dozen red roses –
long stemmed,
drenched in water,
sticking out of a vase
wrapped with shiny gold paper –
you sent to your mother,
mine and me on our first
Valentine's Day.

The lobster, crab, shrimp
and cheddar biscuits,
the lamb gyros, cucumber
sauce and Pita bread
in the Seafood and Greek
restaurants where we celebrated
over the decades.

Trips to Albuquerque
and Sedona
where you bought me
turquoise and crystals.

But what I love best
is when you pluck
a wayward balloon
saying *I love You*
from the cholla cactus
and sing Happy Valentine's
Day in your tenor voice

and you broil lobster
and serve it in melted
butter with a baked potato
and we sit at the dining
room table and watch
the deer and doves
at the waterfalls
as the sun sets over
the Elephant Rock.

I Am Waiting For My Sweet and Sour Shrimp

at the Chinese Dragon
Café when I study
The Chinese Zodiac
on the placemat.

And discover I am
a water horse
with the spirit
of self sacrifice.

Married to a bold
courageous
and faithful fire dog
and we are parents

of an earth rooster
with a pragmatic
personality, a wood
tiger who plays pranks.

A charming charismatic
fire dragon and giving
but too trusting
earth horse.

I find it as reliable
as the fortune cookie

which reads; *You have*
a secret admirer.

Still, I secretly stash
the sauce stained
paper mat and fortune
in my purse for safe keeping.

His Chips Come with Cod

delicious
deep fried
wrapped
in newspapers
and sold in shops
in the sixties
throughout Scotland
summer and winter.

He is nineteen
when he travels
by bus, train
and bicycle
from the beaches
where the breeze
from the bay
caresses his skin
like a Scottish lass

to the mountains
where his face
is slapped
by the wind
from the Artic
Circle
like a jealous
rival.

Renting a room
from families
who teach
him the Scottish
brogue,
feed him
boiled brussel
sprouts and mince
and introduce
him to James Bond
on television

At the Highland
Games
he watches
men in kilts
marching
and playing
bag pipes
and drums

and wrestling
with members
of other clans
figuring
some
are relatives
since his ancestors
came from
Norway.

Sometimes Life is an Action Movie

He drives his Chevy
one ton camper
with the kids
in the back
on the dirt road
in the mid eighties.

The pretty brunette
flags him down,
shows him
her shredded tire.
Says she is filming
a movie in Florence
and needs a ride
to the set.

She introduces him
to her co-star
who plays her husband,
a convenience store
robber with bushy
hair, eyebrows,
mustache and Elvis
sideburns.

The next day he reads
in the newspaper
they shut the whole
town down to film

the robber leading
the sheriff on a car chase.

It isn't until he watches
the movie, *Raising*
Arizona, that he recognizes
the woman he rescued
as Holly Hunter,
and the man who shook
his hand as Nicholas Cage.

He's Not a Gambling Man

So he doesn't drop
a dime in the slot
machines at Circus
Circus Casino
in Las Vegas

with young kids
when a plate filled
with ham and eggs
and hashbrowns
cost 99 cents.

He slips a quarter
in a slot machine
at Agua Caliente Casino
in Palm Springs
after we get free water

on a sizzling summer day
and three cherries
wins $50 which buys
a lobster dinner
for the both of us.

He resists the hunger
for cherries and oranges
spinning and falling
when we spot Cousin
Susan's sleek sedan

in the parking lot
of Desert Diamond Casino
in Tucson and stop
to save her from spending
all her cash on Blackjack.

At Virgin River Hotel
and Casino in Mesquite
he watches football
on the big screen TV
as smoke swirls

around slot machines
sucking up coins and bills
after the air conditioner
fails in the motel room
in triple digit temperatures.

For his 65th birthday
he bellies up to the buffet
at Apache Gold Casino
In Globe, just a few miles
from home and as he leaves

stops in at the casino
and plops a quarter
in the closest slot
for old time sake
and loses to a fruit salad.

Our Oldest Son is a Self-Proclaimed Redneck

He even says so
on his Facebook page
which contains
cartoons of Maxine
mouthing off :
I'd trace my family tree
but it raises mostly nuts,
and a cow bellowing:
Born to be wild
until about 9 pm.

Not to mention the video
of Cowboy Butter Steak Sliders
grilled over the open fire
and the recipe for Redneck
Turtle Burgers wrapped
in s shell of bacon
with hot dogs
for legs and tails.

Don't forget the flag
flying in his yard
and his military medals
on his uniform hanging
in the hallway closet.

And all the machines
he designs and puts together

in his shop and sells
on the internet
when he is not in his semi
delivering food and supplies.

With Six Grandsons Behind the Wheel

The call we dread
but fear we're
going to get comes
while we're eating
popcorn and watching
television in the evening.

It's our oldest son
just turned fifty.
I hear sadness
in his voice
and clutch my cell
phone like a raft.

I gasp for air
as he speaks
of a car collision,
our second oldest
grandson in a coma
in an ICU, a machine
breathing for him.

I see the baby
with chubby cheeks
and curls turn into
a tall twenty-five-
year-old reciting
his vows in a suit
just three months ago.

My heart is broken,
I say as my son
and his father go silent.
I wish I could
change places with him.
But all I can do is wait.

On his fifth day in ICU,
we get another call.
This time his mother
shouts, *He's breathing*
on his own and opened
one eye and said,
What's up Mama?

Past Life

On the Fourth of July

my father is born
to English and poetry
teachers who name
him after the poet
Ralph Waldo Emerson.

Although he takes
dangerous detours
riding freight trains,
broncs and bulls,
teaching English
is his first love.

His second love
is cooking gourmet
meals in cafes,
but his fire cracker
temper flares
and gets him fired.

Once his temper almost
lands him in jail
when a principal
of a school on an Indian
Reservation watches

my father walking
with a rifle after a shouting
match in his office

and tells the sheriff
my father is hiring
a hitman to murder him.

Two deputies find my father
in the only bar showing off
his hunting rifle and pheasant
to his Native American
drinking buddies. No charges

are filed but the school board
fails to hire him for another year
and he moves on to another
school hard up for teachers.

Father Knows Best

My father is sitting
at his desk grading papers
and eating a Snickers
while waiting for his ride

after faculty and students
with bad grades,
attitudes and tempers
have left the middle school

for broken homes, part
time jobs or friends
when he hears footsteps
on the stairs and a scrawny

guy with glasses sticks
his head in the door
and says, *Gordy and his boys*
are coming to kill you.

Go call the cops, my father
says as tires squeal
on the pavement and boots
pound down the hallway.

With one arm shriveled
from shrapnel in the war,
my fifty something father
channels his younger cowboy.

Tackles the three teen
football stars and disarms
them one by one
and has them hogtied

and in a pile with his foot
on the chest of the biggest
by the time the cops show up
with guns and handcuffs.

After the front page newspaper
headlines hail him a hero,
the hoots and hollers,
high fives and fist bumps

fly the way of my father
and for the rest of the school year
my father's students are obedient
while his attackers stew in jail.

It Feels Normal to Me

Daddy disappearing
after school is out
on Memorial Day
and not returning
until he spends
every cent of the check
that was supposed
to put food on the table
and a roof over our head.

Showing up
with whisky breath
and a knapsack
full of cash
he wins
playing poker
in the pool halls.

Gathering
the cash
jumping
on my bicycle
and riding
to the landlord's house,
the power company
and the grocery store
that gives us credit
to pay the bills.

But one summer Labor
Day comes and goes
and daddy is not home.
My police chief uncle
searches the drunk
tanks and hospitals
and morgues
all over the state
and no daddy.

Mama tells
the principal
daddy
has pneumonia
and the school
hires a substitute.

Meanwhile,
the bill collectors
and landlord knock
on our door, leaving past
due notices on the porch.

When the Welfare Lady
comes calling, Mama
gets testy and throws
her off the property.
He's away on a road trip,
she says, and I believe
she believes it so I do.

A friend of Uncle Jack
says he spots Daddy

cooking in a café
in a hotel
across the state
and gives him
the address.

Mama writes:
Get home., You have
a family to feed.

I wake up
one morning
and see Daddy
smiling
and sober
at the breakfast
table drinking coffee
and eating ham
and eggs
in his suit and tie.

Mama hands
me money
to pay the bills.
I ride off
on my bicycle
and daddy drives
to school
and we all act
like he was
never gone
in the first place
like we always did.

My father is Not Himself

After he loses
his balance
while standing
on the desk
in his bookstore
while changing
a lightbulb
and falls
and breaks
his hip.

After hardware
is installed
in the hospital
he is back
behind the desk
and recalling
the plot
of every
best seller
on his shelves –
from Sheldon
to Sagan
to Spillane.

He entertains
customers
with favorite
lines like

at home
with my sister
and me
when he recited
Wordsworth,
Dickinson
and Frost

and inspires
students
with Shakesperean
Soliloquies
and tragedies,
only a memory

as he shuffles
through the store
straightening
the spines
on the books
resembling Charles
Dickens in his long
white hair and beard.

Mama was Queen of Hearts

Her heart was as big
as the state of Montana
and her ratted hair.

Definitely not Queen
of Diamonds or Clubs
Maybe Queen of Spades.

Daddy couldn't afford
diamonds but she loved
her dime store jewelry.

She never joined a club
because she was not
a social butterfly,

Preferring spading her
garden, doing housework
and taking care of us.

Rolling Pin in Hand

My mother answers
the door in her apron,
nose powdered with flour.
I recognize the voices
of two senior girls.

We don't get visitors
this late at night so she
tells my sister and I to stay
in our bedrooms while
she talks to them through
the screen door.

The girls who snicker
and taunt me at school.
ask for me in a sugary voice
as if we are best friends.

My mother asks what
they want with me.
It's Freshman Initiation,
the leader of the pack says.

That was banned when
q freshman was paralyzed
after he was pushed
off the cliff by a senior,
my mother says in a firm voice.

The school says we can do
it with the permission
of a parent, the girls
chorus. You're not
getting my permission
to brutalize my child.
Now go home to bed.
It's a school night.

They are speechless
and silent as mother
closes the front door.
Although my mother
is usually nice and polite
and smiles at strangers,
when it comes to protecting
her cubs, my mother
is a fierce lioness.

A Saphire and an Emerald

After my father dies,
a gray haired rock
hunter and jeweler
with a grisly beard
brings my mother
an Emerald on a gold
band and me a Saphire
set in a silver band.

Maybe he's got money
and no survivors, I say,
suggesting I should marry
him when mother says:
*I will marry him, M*y jaw
drops because my mother
does not crack jokes.

She was married to my father
forever. It was the first time
I realized my mother was free
to marry but she never does
and we never see the man
again but the rings are both
still in her jewelry box
two decades after her death.

The Day My Mother Takes on Terrorists

My mother, an eighty-year-old widow,
calls me on the phone on a Sunday
evening and she is so hysterical
I can't understand her. All I can make
out is the thugs that had been
terrorizing the neighborhood
peopled with senior citizens
for months had stolen something
and were dismembering it.
I cringe thinking it is the stray
cat I'd been feeding behind
the building. *Call 911*, I say,
I'm on my way. I drive across town
and arrive in time to see two
teenagers in handcuffs and a tow
truck lifting a Harley Davidson
out of the stairwell at the apartment
house next door to the bookstore.
The detective is taking my mother's
statement. She says she had looked out
her bedroom window above
the bookstore and saw two boys
stealing the motorcycle owned
by her neighbor who was on vacation.
She hurried down the stairs
and told them to put it back,
It doesn't belong to you, she says
she told them and points at the teenagers
in handcuffs. She adds, *but they didn't*

mind me and wheeled it right past me.
The detective calls my mother
a hero and the thieves call
her a liar and snitch and the B word
and tell her to watch her back.
My mother tells the felons
she will bring them cookies in jail.
Even bad boys need to eat, she says
as she walks upstairs to watch *Dallas*
while they ride off in the police car.

I Should Have Been Born a Bull Instead of a Ram, My Mother Says

I was due
on April 23
but arrived
a month early
on March 27
and my cousin Sue
booked my due date.

Sue kept her feet
on earth,
but belonged
on Venus,
the planet
of pleasure.

Wore
a diamond
and daisies
when she wed
the boy next
door due
to a swollen
belly
at fifteen.

And stayed
in a loveless
marriage,

bearing three
more sons
until two decades
later she met
and married
her true love.

While I wore red,
and aquamarine gems,
picked dandelions
and rubbed them
under my chin
until it was yellow
as butter.

Longed to live
on Mars,
and climb
mountains,
was drawn
to fire and cardinals.

And flew solo
with a parachute
on my back
until I met my match,
a Lion born in July.

Mama and Me

The woman
in the photo
smiles,
spine straight,
not one hair
out of place,
lips and eyebrows
colored
within the lines.

I stare, squint,
slouch, scowl,
with bed hair,
eyebrows
a question mark,
lips naked
as a newborn.

Mama
steps out
of the frame
straightens
me up,
corrects
my shortcomings
and cleans up
my messes.

I am a Bad Singer

But I always wished
I could sing like Mama
and lip synced and sang
along to the radio
pretending I was performing
onstage at the CMAs.

Now I pretend those teens
and twenty somethings
singing, strumming
and swiveling their hips
on voice competitions
are my grandchildren.

I'm a little partial
to the crooners in hats,
boots and fringes
singing Johnny, Elvis,
Willy, Dolly and Patsy
with a twang and a guitar.

I clap and cheer and cross
my fingers that they will
win and my heart breaks
when they don't just like
their blood grandma
and other adopted
grandmas like me.

I Eat Hot Roast Beef Sandwiches

With scoops
of mashed potatoes
and gravy
on soft bread

At the casino
where the Greyhound
carrying me
from Billings
to Idaho Falls
stopped
in the forties.

In the dining car
in the train traveling
from Billings
to Butte
to Idaho Falls
in the fifties
and sixties.

But in the jets flying
from San Francisco
to Los Angeles
in the seventies
the beef and potatoes
were dehydrated
and steamed.

The last time we flew
from Arizona to Idaho
in the 2000s
all we were offered
was cocktails, coke
and a bag of peanuts.

At Woolworth's Soda Fountain in the Fifties

In bobbysocks
and saddle shoes,
my sister and I
sit on swivel stools
with our widowed
grandmother
in her fox stole
scarfing down
fifty cent
toasted triple decker
bacon and tomato
sandwiches,
thirty nine cent
banana splits
with three scoops
of ice cream,
chocolate syrup
and whipped cream
and wash it down
with a twenty five
cent malted milk
while my father
sits on a bar stool
on skid row
blowing his paycheck
on booze and poker
and mother waits
at home
drinking coffee
in her dime store
jewelry and dress.

Nancy Drew Teaches Me to Snoop and Sleuth

But the secrets
I hear
on the telephone
party lines
at the houses
where I babysit
give me enough
stories to scoop
the scandal sheets.
Not wanting to blow
my cover, I keep
my mouth shut
and create fictional
characters on paper
and hide them
in the closet
until I hear
the Queen of Mean
confess
she is sleeping
with the boyfriend
of my best friend.

I am not a Bouvier

and did not marry
a senator
who became
president
of the United States,
but I must confess
I have her dark eyes,
bouffant brown hair,
bushy eyebrows
cherry cheekbones
and sleek body
in silhouette
sleeveless dresses,
which is why
a photo of me
wins first place
in the national
Jacqueline Kennedy
Look Alike Contest
when I am nineteen.

In a Billings Bar March 6, 1963

I bawl in my beer
as a Patsy Cline
wannabe sings
'She's Got You."

In his black hat,
boots and belt
with a silver dollar
in his buckle,

the red faced cowboy,
slides in the booth beside
me, swigging suds
as the buxom brunette wails:

I've got the records, that we used to share
And they still sound the same as when you were here
The only thing different, the only thing new
I've got the records ... she's got you.

I can't believe she's dead,
I say as he orders a pitcher.
Who? he asks. *Patsy Cline.*
I say. *Who's that?* he asks.

I show him the Gazette front page.
Patsy Cline Dead in Plane Crash.
He spills his beer on his shirt.
You didn't just get dumped?

I laugh. *I can't remember how long*
that's been. When the pitcher comes,
he slips away and my fellow reporters
pay the waiter and join me in the booth

during the break as Patsy's voice pours
out of the juke box, *I'm crazy for feeling*
so lonely. I'm crazy for feeling so blue
and somehow the sorrow subsides.

Shirts

While he plays
racquetball
in his sweats,
she tosses
his dozen shirts
in the laundromat dryer
and then rushes off
to Smitty's Café
to meet her sister
for lunch and then
home to clean house
and cook dinner.

She doesn't remember
the shirts until she slides
the casserole and cake
in the oven. She searches
the laundromat
but the shirts have vanished.
Socks, sheets and blankets
spin in the dryer where
the sheets once swirled.

Married just six months,
she imagines him handing
her divorce papers
as she finds the stores
where he buys his shirts

closed and her bank
account on empty.

Smoke billows and flames
crackle as they drive up,
she in her yellow bug
and he in his VW wagon
just as the fire truck arrives.
Her tears flow so fast
they flood the flowers
in the pots and the garden
as she gulps, *Shirts gone.*

He holds her close and says,
We can always buy more
shirts. At least we have
each other, as they eat
burgers and fries. It isn't
until their 50th anniversary
that she confesses the shirts
didn't burn up in the fire.

Baby Breath

Beloved beautiful niece,
a half century ago I watched
you take your first breath
of the salty sea in Sausalito

on a chilly December day
as the firemen delivered
you from my sister's womb
in the house on the hill.

You watched your twins -
a daughter blonde
like you - and son -
dark haired like his father –

take their first breaths
of sea air in San Francisco
and Maui where they ride
the waves in the wind.

And someday, maybe
even after I stop breathing,
you will watch
your grandchildren

take their first breaths
and hold them as long
as they can above
and below water.

The Wailing Woman

Sobs awaken me
at midnight
as I sleep soundly
in my flat
in the Portuguese
District in Toronto.

The kind of wailing
from a widow
of a fallen soldier
or a woman
with an empty womb.

I stare at the ceiling
for what seems like hours
wondering which floor,
which wall she weeps behind.
Then I hear only silence.

The next morning a woman
in a scarf speaking broken
English knocks on my door.
I search for streaked
mascara or mud puddles
but see only smooth skin.

A woman pulls a suitcase
down the stairs smiling
silently. I see no black

clouds in her blue sky
eyes as she hails a cab
bound for the airport.

Who died? Who broke
Your heart? I want to ask
all the females I meet
in the hallway or street
but I don't because
the wailing woman
could be any of us, even me.

Burn Butter on Buns, my Fitness Trainer Says

As we squeeze,
squat and step up,
shimmy, shake and shuffle,
press, pump and pushup,

my rack of ribs
is smothered
with sauce,
seasoned

and grilled
from rare
to medium
to well-done.

Muscles, bones
and breasts
boil in broth
until tender.

Fairly fat free,
I am served up
sizzling and steamy
on a platter.

The Oil of Olay Salesman Stops in my Shop

not to buy books but to sell me
cream to keep my skin soft
and smooth and supple
but saves his spiel when he sees
me then in my forties wearing
the skin of a twenty-year-old
as I sit at my desk eating a salad.

I think it's from drinking water
all day long as I write novels
between selling books to customers.
His eye is on the bottle of virgin
olive oil which I pour on the greens.
That's the main ingredient
in our creams, he says.

I realize he is right when as a senior
I forgo salads drenched in olive oil
for cherry and pumpkins pies
and chocolate chip cookies.
My skin dries up like the desert
in a drought. Old age, I think.

I drench my lizard like skin
in moisturizers but it remains
dry and chapped until I resume
my salad and olive oil routine
and my skin is again smooth,
soft and supple as the desert
after a flash flood.

Writing Life

The 40th Academy Awards in 1968

As a girl growing up
in a tiny Montana town
I dream of being Katherine
and Audrey Hepburn
and winning an Oscar
at the Academy Awards.

Even though the naysayers
tell me I'll never leave
the city limits of Columbus,
here I am entertainment editor
for a newspaper thirty
miles from Hollywood
opening an invitation
to the Oscars where Katherine
and Audrey are nominated
for the Best Actress award.

I gladly accept, believing
I will get to meet and interview
my idols, only to find out
the press would not be
in the audience, but watching
from a close circuit television
behind the scenes. I am livid.
Why would I dress up and fight
traffic and parking problems
when I could watch from home.

So I pass up the opportunity,
one of those decisions
I regret five decades later
and five hundred miles
from Hollywood
as I watch the 96th
Academy Awards, giving
anything to be backstage
just a few feet from Jodie
Foster and Jessica Lange,
the only actresses whose
movies I remember.

In San Miguel de Allende

in the seventies
with no phones,
radios or TV
and few cars,

I walk a mile
on cobble streets
to learn to write
fiction at the Instituto.

Live behind blue walls
and a locked gate
with Ursula from Sweden
who sculptures statues,

Fred from Philadelphia
who paints abstracts
and the Spanish
students from Nigeria.

Sit in the square
listening to church
bells chime, devour
huevos rancheros

and tacos and beans,
and soak in the Hot
Springs with writers,
Ralph, Bob and Ivan.

Fall asleep to Mariachi.
music and bullfights
and wake up to the chorus
of street dogs and roosters.

The Muse Rides a Harley

into her driveway just as the sky
fades from tar to eggshell blue,
jarring her awake like a jackhammer.
Through the window, she watches him
peel off his helmet and leather jacket,
notices the ocean wave has receded

from his hairline and sand has settled
on his midriff since he disappeared. She tries
to tell him she doesn't need him anymore,
but he finds prepositions hanging with bath
towels, misplaced metaphors in the silverware
drawer, participles dangling from the balcony.

Over brandy in front of the hearth, he apologizes
and promises he'll never leave again.
She invites him to move into the guest room.
As the sky turns crimson, they discuss allusion
and anthropomorphism while tossing shrimp
and crab leg shells to the swooping gulls.

As they dance to the rhythm of bat wings
beating time, he whispers alliteration and allegory.
He paints bumblebees sipping nectar from long-
stemmed tulip glasses on a hallway mural.
Cacophony and hyperbole caterwaul as she writes
under full moon and scalding sun.

One day she realizes the guest room is empty.
As she reads her poems and signs autographs,
she expects to see him smiling in the crowd.
On mountain trails and at the shore, she searches
for him, but finds him in the garden planting
metaphors and similes under a turquoise sky.

The Muse Speaks

I've been pounding on her door
and ringing her doorbell
until my hands hurt
so I check to make sure the address
is correct and peer through the window
and recognize the poetess
from her photo. The door opens
and she flies past me pushing
the buttons on her remote
and as the doors unlock on her Nissan,
I slip in the back seat. I sing syllables
and synonyms but she can't hear me
over Sting screaming from the radio.
She pulls into Starbucks and I follow
whispering wise words in her ear.
but she is too busy blabbing
on her cellphone as she orders
a cold brew expresso. At the park,
we sit side by side on the bench
and I point to a cardinal
flaming like fire, ducklings
swimming in the stream, clouds
swirling like sheets on the line,
but she is on Facebook posting
likes, loves and emojis.
Just when I give up on her,
I see her pull out her pen
and notebook and scribble
a line or two and I smile
and scurry off to save my next poet.

To all You Vicenarians and Tricenarians

Who may
think you
monopolize
the market
on poetry.
Watch out
for us
sexagenarians,
septuagenarians,
octogenarians
and nonagenarian,
who despite cancer,
heart attacks,
macular degeneration
and arthritis
still write
verse
on notebooks,
computers
and cell phones
from hospital beds,
cars or planes
knowing the muse
won't stop
whispering
in our ear
until we draw
our last breath.

The Invitation Reads:

You are invited to a poetry reading,
with a tempting trail that leads
to the gingerbread, cake and candy
house forbidden by my Diabetes Doctor.

Don't go down that road, a voice
whispers. But like Hansel and Gretel
I skip down the lane and find myself
in a familiar land of storytellers

whose heads lie face down
on their computer keys. A voice
says: *When the host calls your name*
you will awaken and recite your poem.

When my name is called my head
is heavy and my mouth moves
but no words flow out. *Unmute*
yourself, the host hollers.

Best to not bother her. She is probably.
writing another poem, Marianne mumbles.
Sharon can make a poem out of anything,
Shoshauna sings. *A poem writes itself.*

Everyone knows that, Jim joins in. I feel
a tap on my shoulder. *You fell asleep*
at the computer again, my husband
informs. Storyteller Land disappears.

I am a Portrait of the Women in my Past

at the zoom poetry reading
as I stare at the computer
screen with Grandma Anna's
dark eyes and mouth words
with Mama's red Revlon lips
and cross the long lanky
legs of Grandma Emma.

I wear Mama 's pearl necklace
and Anna's sensible shoes
with the purple pullover
of mama-in-law Phyllis
and gray slacks like Grandma
Emma. That's where
the similarities end.

School teacher Anna's long
white tresses would coil in a bun.
Mama's thick auburn curls
would pile high on her head.
Grandma Emma's silver helmet
would be short and sleek.
And Phyllis's gray hair would
be clipped and curled
close to her face.

My silver and gold hair
billows down my back
to my waist in waves

as I recite their stories
in free verse long after
they've lived their lives
and left legacies to me.

I Schedule a Zoom Poetry Reading on Super Bowl Sunday

Realize my mistake
from the messages.
Sorry, nothing could
stop me but football.
Cooking chili
at the big bash
for hubby and boys.

Others say: *I'll be there*
so we don't re-schedule.
Then there's the last
minute cancelations.
My back went out.
I have laryngitis.
Pacemaker operation.

It's like the birthday
parties where you wonder
if anyone will show up
and then there they are
all those faces popping
up on the screen with smiles
as bright as balloons.

There we are on YouTube

A dozen faces glowing
in the dark like fireflies
wiping tears smiling
laughing clapping
as we read our stories
about sassafras and sugar
a filly and stallion
a mob of kangaroos
homesickness
supermarkets and yogurt
saint without a history
pain, patience and peace
cocky little chin toss
sweet short sugary house
skittering spider
unbuckled shoes
blue balcony
and rocket blasts
and then return
to our lives in Australia,
South America, India,
Canada and the USA.

The Morning of the Zoom

I wake up and the desert
rat that built a nest under
the hood of the Camaro
parked in the garage
must have nested in my hair.

The brush balks
and I fear I will show
up at the poetry reading
wearing a beehive
or a haystack on my head.

But after shampooing
and shaping, strands
slink smoothly across
my shoulders and down
my back like a model
on the runway.

But Zoom refuses me entry.
I go to email the hostess
and a dozen emails echo
the same plight. *Can't get in.*
I fixed it, she writes.

I like how I look onscreen
in the tiny little cubicle
until I watch it on YouTube.
My face cracks and crumbles
like a cavern while my voice
shouts and echoes but a stream
of blonde hair flows freely
with no snags or snarls.

Don't Write a Poem About Me

My mother-in-law says sternly
but I write enough to fill a book
and when I read them to her,
she smiles, especially
in her last days when the poems
distract her from the pain.

My mother says I won a contest
with a poem, *Elvis Presley's*
Pink Cadilac, when I was a teen.
But I don't remember.
She is long gone before I write
poems about her and daddy
but I know she wouldn't mind.

Don't write a poem about me,
my husband says after I've been
writing poems about him
for two decades. I laugh.
Who else would I write about?
I say. Everyone else is gone.

Sister Poets

Our voices carry
from the seaside, desert,
mountains and jungle
as we write stories
short and strong
as our names:

Jayne, Joan, Fran,
Sarah, Donna, Tina,
Judy, Lori, Mary,
Holly, Kelly, Peggy,
Betsy, and Robbi.

Melodies musical
as Marianne, Marilyn,
Margaret, Mary Ellen,
Rose Mary, Tamara,
Jacqueline, Joanne,
Cynthia and Barbara.

Alliteration as lilting
as Laurie, Lauren, Laura,
Lynn, Lorraine and Luane
and Arlene and Angela.

Language unique
as Abha, Alarie, Carolynn,
Kavita, Wilda, Rachael,
Shaun and Shoshauna.

Brother Poets

We sister poets harmonize
with our poet brothers
with names my parents
may have chosen.
had they gifted me
with brothers smart,
funny and talented

as Alan, Ethan, Joe,
Jim, John, Gary
Martin, Mike, Neil.
Paul and Steven.

When I was a child,
I dreamed of growing
up in Australia cuddling
kangaroos and koala bears
with a brother who reads
me poetry in an Ausie accent.

When Neil reads poetry
as kangaroos hop
outside his window
I swoon like a groupie
at an Elvis concert.

She's a Rambler

Not all those who wander are lost; The old that is strong does not wither, Deep roots are not reached by the frost. JRR Tolkien

Sentences tumble
over her tongue
as she talks,
writes poetry
and travels
all over Europe.

She sends me
postcards
from Venice
puckering up
to a performer
saying, *I had*
to slap him.
He was fresh
but fun.

From Antigua,
with her hubby,
knee deep in water
holding stingrays
like colorful fans.

From Honduras,
cuddling Charley,
the female sloth

who wraps
arms around her
neck like a baby.

From the Blue Lagoon,
a dolphin kissing her
cheek like a child
as she swims with hubby.

We travel for the kids,
she says. Me and Mike
since we don't have any.
Our cats are our children
We hire a sitter
while we're gone.

Even at sixty-six she's
still booking two trips
a year. She feels
the urgency to do it now
before the MS worsens
or the cancer comes back.

Corresponding with Barbara Crooker

She pens poetry
about Van Gogh
and romancing
a chemist in Rome.

I scribble poems
about marrying
a cowboy who sings
Willie Nelson songs.

After buying her books
in Barnes and Noble,
and reading her work
on Writers Almanac,

I send her a fan email
expecting an automated
reply, but instead receive
a warm letter and soon

we two grandmothers
are chatting
about the simple life
of the sixties, when

tips from serving
thirty-cent burgers
at the drive-in paid
for college tuition.

Pushing Eighty-Six from Peru

The poet peers at the screen
through round rimmed glasses
and white spider web strands
on her forehead and recites
her poem, *Sunsets on Mars*
Are Blue, sharing the screen
with the poem *because I can.*
Her mischievous smile
sparking a ripple of laughter
as the camera zooms.
She says she is not afraid
of death since flatlining
during surgery for a brain
tumor. Still, she agrees
to installation of a pacemaker
in her heart. *Now I won't*
die peacefully in my sleep
or when I'm walking down
the street unless a flower
pot falls on my head, she says.
Meanwhile she take life
one poem at a time.

The Daughters I Never Raised

When the doctors say: *You lost*
the baby, I don't believe them.
I imagine she has been stolen
and we will reunite someday
like those mothers in the movies
and on missing children documentaries.

I love your poetry, the blonde
forty-eight-year-old comments
on the site of a journal where
I publish poetry as a senior citizen.
She sends her poems, short stories
and photos. *You have my smile*
and cheekbones and got your writing
talent from me, I want to say.
I'm sure I've found my lost child.

Now I have to find her sister.
She shows up not long after.
A beautiful fifty something
with my brown eyes, dark hair
and personality. A perfectionist.
Over achiever. Like me, she writes
novels as a child and starts
writing poetry after the age of fifty.

Do you have any children?
they ask, but of course,
they already know since
they are psychic like me.

Happy Birthday, Sharon, She Sings

in a soprano songbird voice
from San Francisco on her son's
cellphone as her granddaughters
chirp like canaries in the background.
I tell her I saw her at the zoom
poetry reading sitting on a chair
wearing her white hair
like a crown as her granddaughters,
dark-eyed, brown skinned like her,
run in and out of view, leaning
on her lap and holding onto her arm
knowing she will fly back to India
out of touch and sight soon.
She says she saw me coughing
and drinking a beverage.
I hope it was hot and soothed
your throat, she says. Before she
hangs up she promises she
will call me on my next birthday
when she is back in San Francisco,
and I say, *I'd love that*, both of us
clinging to the hope that will happen.

The Poet at Ninety

Blind now,
she still creates
stories
of life with
Ma and Pa
and the love
of her life,
all gone now,
in her home
in Wisconsin
she shares
with a daughter.

Dictates poems
to her I-Pad,
memorizes
and reads
her poetry
on zoom,
and still
publishes books,
something she
never dreamed
of doing

as a 12-year-old
girl in Wisconsin
during World War II,
as an English

teacher
or even when
she penned
her first poem
at seventy-two
and published
her first poem
at seventy-seven.

After publishing
her fifth book
of poetry
she tells
The Spectator
Ted Kooser
is her inspiration.
I write simple,
no beating
around the bush.

Catfish Messages me on Facebook

I spent 4 days at the Milwaukee VA Hospital.
Not Covid, nor the flu, nor SRV, some weird virus.
At least I'm home, crawling around.
Happy Holidaze. Adios Cat

The last message I got from the Beatnik
poet was in the summer when I told
him I was so booked up I couldn't
publish his poems for a year:

You're 81 and I just turned 70.
My mom died at 61 and my father at 71
and my younger sisters are dead.
Hope we both are alive next July.

I tell him: *I'm sure we will be.* Now
I am not so sure. I bump him up
telling him that my dad died of a virus
at my age and I thought I was dying last night.

Thanks Shar, he writes.
I hope to be above ground
and not corpse dust. by then.
Hang tough. Word Lady. Adios Cat

I have a feeling there's more
to the story. *Got tests back*
today, he writes: *Heart attack.*
I reply: *Soldier On* and he does.

We Hear His Voice but Don't See His Face

at the zoom poetry reading
in November. The Vietnam Vet
says he is calling from a bed
in a hospital in Denver.

I haven't shaved in days,
You don't want to see me,
he jokes and laughs as he reads
about Bangkok in the seventies.

He misses the December zoom.
Still in the hospital, he writes,
Finished chemo for the cancer.
Now I'm undergoing radiation.

He's a no show at the January
and February zoom and I wonder
why his wife isn't answering
my emails and giving me updates.

In late February he emails, *Still*
in Denver for outpatient treatment.
My wife of 52 years died
two days before Thanksgiving.

In her Sixties, The Poet Shares Secrets in a Tell-All Book

She confesses
to sending
Valentines

and holding
clients on laps
as they talk.

Getting hurt,
heartbroken
and dumped.

You fall in love
and they kick
the bucket.

And she may
be the last
to know.

Bumping into
their loved ones
at the store.

It's all part
of her job
as a cat sitter.

I stare at the fat
feral cat curled
up in our sun porch

and am grateful
for the glass
that separates us.

Present Life with Al

Dancing With a Scorpion

Me in two bare feet, he in six feet,
we two step, tap dance and shuffle
to the beat of my drumming heart
when we meet at midnight,

the glowing night light
guiding us as we glide
across the tile floor. *Quick*
Quick Slow Slow Shuffle Tap.

We repeat the steps, mindful
of the sting and pain if one
of us steps on the other's toes,
until he skitters under the sink.

The Eagles Soar Inside and Out

Two Bald Eagles land
on the waterfalls
and dip their toes
in the cool water

as four hairy Eagles
with guitars rock out,
Peaceful Easy Feeling
from the TV set,

in a documentary
aired after two die
and the others
turn seventy-eight.

As the Bald Eagles hop
down, the hairy Eagles
belt out, *I'm already*
standing on the ground.

By the time the Bald
Eagles flap and fly away,
the hairy Eagles sing,
I'm already gone.

Kenny Rogers Sings *The Gambler*

I sit on a swivel chair
in front of the computer
playing Texas Hold Em
with a pair of twos
trying to decide whether
to check, call, raise or fold
when I see the stranger
in my house muscling
his way down the hallway
in diamonds and tattoos
Kenny sings, *Know when*
to hold and when to fold
but he doesn't say when
to scream. I freeze
and the game sits me out
and the rattlesnake
turns the corner, slithers
past me and heads
for the bathroom
and the toilet bowl.

The French Woman Is on the Phone Again

Every morning
she calls at ten
trying to reach her *mari.*
Voice musical and sad
as a soprano
singing an aria
in a tragic opera in Paris.

I so want to console her
and help her find her love,
but my French is limited
to *Je ne parle pas français*
and each day she gets more
melancholy until her mari
shows up on our doorstep.

Once the telephone lines
are uncrossed, the lovers
are reunited and we hear
her voice no more. I still
miss her sweet song
as soothing as syrup
on a strep throat.

I Hear a Cowgirl Voice

coming from my kitchen
and there she stands, a seventy-
five-year-old gray haired
cowgirl in a cap and sweatshirt
on a chilly day but warm
for the Montana gal who grew
up on the opposite side
of the state as I did.

She says she's been wintering
in Arizona for almost a decade
after her horse trainer husband
was bucked from the back
of a child's pony with bones
that ache in twenty below.

She opens the door to leave
and a blue healer races
past us heels clicking
on the tile, the same dog
my husband says chased
the neighbor's rooster
trespassing on our lawn
before she pulled
up in the driveway.

A Corgi sits passively
on her quad runner
sitting in the driveway

until she whistles
and it runs in circles
at her feet.

They ride up the road
while her husband
waves from his quad
in a motorcade
from the RV Park
where they are staying.

As her wise words
ring in my ears:
As soon as I wake up,
I hit the trails,
Otherwise, I'd be dead
like I thought my husband
was when that pony
tossed him in the air
and left him in the dust.

We Warn the Young Couple From North Dakota

about bobcats, coyotes,
scorpions, tarantulas,
and rattlesnakes
when they pull up
in their motorhome
with the baby and puppy
and park on a lot across
the road last year
and say they are building
a house. We hope
they changed their mind
when we wake up
in the spring
and they are gone.

We are surprised this winter
when we hear a dog barking
and see the motorhome
back on the spot, a toddler
sitting cross-legged
in the dirt digging
with a plastic shovel
and filling her pail
like she is at the beach,
while the mother cradles
her swollen belly
and the father sticks his head
under the hood of his truck.

We listen for cries, screams
and yelps. Hoping that the toddler
doesn't swallow a scorpion,
the dog isn't eaten by a coyote
and the mother's water doesn't
break because cell phones
don't work out here, it's three
miles on a gravel road
to the volunteer fire station
and forty miles to the nearest
hospital. In the spring, we wake
and the spot is empty except
for the pink plastic pail snagged
on a Cholla cactus bush.

Chirps, Chocolate and Cherries

I hear a chirping sound
as I open the freezer door
and defrost the cherries
and melt the chocolate
in the microwave.

But the sound turns
to squawking
as I slice the bananas
and stir in the cashews
and dollop of yogurt.

I hear wings flapping
and see a bird flying
from the bathroom
into the hallway
and behind the open door.

My husband is snoring
away in the guest bedroom
as I eat my sundae
while watching
a documentary on cults.

When he awakens,
I look behind the door.
But the bird has vanished
as if a magician
has waved a scarf.

The Game Camera Shows Sights We Don't See

A herd of javelina
squinting and sniffing
in the darkness
like old ladies with cataracts.

A diamondback dining
on frog legs under
the bench my husband
built with his granddaughter.

A road runner snatching
a rattler and whipping
it around like a lasso
before swallowing it.

A cougar giving birth
behind the brush,
cleaning her cub
with her tongue.

A coyote crouched
behind a Palo Verde
jumping a jackrabbit
jogging along the trail.

A mountain lion running
in the rain between

the wash and the road,
disappearing in the dark.

A hawk swooping in
and scooping up
a squirming squirrel
as it is sky bound.

The feral feline
dropping a dead
packrat on the porch
next to his dish.

The neighbor's
cannibal chickens
feasting on the carcass
of their broasted brother.

A Chicken Strays from the Neighbor's Flock

A coyote follows
the brown hen
from the neighbor's
yard as she traipses
across our property,
breaks her neck
as she bends
to pick up the popcorn
kernel on the ground.

My husband stands
at the window watching
in a blizzard of feathers
as the coyote carries
the dead chicken back
to his den and the rooster
crows a warning:

Predator in our Midst
as the sun rises in the valley
just like the warning
we gave our neighbors
when they got the chickens
and let them roam
in the wildlife habitat.

The neighbor wagged
her finger as she does now
when she sees the feathers

covering our lawn. *It's your*
fault my chicken is dead,
she says. You lured coyotes
with your water. And my
chickens with your snacks.

We close the door knowing
reasoning with her is like
trying to convince a hungry
coyote to stop dining
on the smorgasbord of squirrels,
chipmunks and chickens,
fearing the feral feline is next.

Guess Who is Squatting in the Sunroom?

My husband wakes up
from his afternoon nap
to a bang in the Arizona
room so he looks through
the window expecting
to see the feral orange tabby
he has been feeding
for over a year.

Instead, a gray spotted Bobcat
twice the size of the domestic
cat sprawls across the air
conditioner sniffing scents
and traces the steps
of the cat we call Survivor
as he jumps on a chair,
stands on the top
of the dining room table
and slips through the slit
in the screen door and sun
bathes on the scaffold.
in the courtyard until sundown.

The cat dish is empty
and Survivor is MIA.
There's the usual suspects:
the bobcat, coyotes, dogs.

Then the unlikely suspects:
a cougar, a bear or maybe
he ran off and is in hiding.
Time will tell the truth.

The Cat and the Coyote

My husband sees the feral
tabby on the front lawn
washing his face
after a breakfast
of raw turkey meatballs.

Suddenly the cat's fur
sticks out like quills
of a porcupine
and his back hunches
and his claws come out
as they both see a cunning
coyote creeping closer
to the hissing cat.

The coyote vamooses
like a scared rabbit
when my hero
steps out on the porch.
The cat chews out
the man who feeds him.
Seems to be saying:
Stop trying to fight
my battles. I had this.
As if he's been here.
Done this before.
Which is why
we call him Survivor.

The Mousetrap is Missing

from the kitchen counter
my husband discovers
as he brews his coffee.

He hears clattering
and clomping
on the tile

as a mouse drags
the trap behind him
like a heavy suitcase.

Sees the trap containing
the mouse tail tipped
on its side outside

a cupboard while
the mouse is inside
making mischief.

While my husband
grabs a giant glove
to pick up the trap

and captor, the crafty
culprit makes its getaway
and the game of Man

and Mouse or Catch
A Mouse by the Tail
continues for ten days

until we hear a clacking
noise in the living room
and see the trap bouncing

on the tile and my husband
grabs the trap and carries
it outside and releases the mouse.

Why We don't Walk Barefoot in the House

The creature I see
as I sit at the computer
is shadowlike, small
like a mouse.
Speedy like a road
runner or lizard.

One second it stands
there and then it
vanishes. Maybe it flew.
Could be a hawk, he says.

A hawk would not fly
inside the house, I say.
It was in the house?
Yes, you saw it.

Said it was skinny
like a spider,
skittered under
the dresser.

It's gone now.
We don't know
how they get in
or get out.

The Lawn Mowers

The green grass grows
day after day as the rain
pours down in pitchers
and still the lawn mowers
don't show up. *I saw them*
on the highway, my husband
says, *They'll be here soon.*
We watch and wait as the grass
grows thick and tall. Finally
my husband makes a call
in the evening. *My lawn*
needs mowing, he says.
We wake up to mooing
and bellowing and the cows
chewing the grass
And by noon they've mowed
the lawn on all the acres.

Snow Swirls in the Sky

Like vanilla softies
served on a tray
at The Tastee-Freez
by carhops on roller
skates in the fifties

Hail covers the ground like ice
chips scooped and stuffed
in a cup by my granddaughter
at the Snow Shack in the suburbs
of Salt Lake City in the summer.

It's January, but our bodies
are used to being basted,
barbecued and baked
like sizzling steaks
in the Arizona desert.

Sounds and Sights of Summer

As night falls
owl wonders who

will survive while
coyotes yip as they hunt

and cougars, bobcats
creep on soft socks.

At dawn, red rooster
wakes up the flock.

Quail, doves, wrens
twitter and tweet.

Horses whinny for hay.
Cows bellow for water.

Flicker knocks on wood.
Diamondback rattles its tail.

Deer dance day and night
as water falls over the rocks.

As temperatures rise, it's
silent as it is Siesta time.

When the sun sets again,
scorpions and spiders sleep.

The javelina soak and swim
like dolphins in the pond

as the bumblebees' buzzers
are put on snooze and bats

wake up and whiz and waltz
with moths and mosquitos.

Trading Trains for Tarantulas

In my thirties,
I jump out of bed
and into the shower
and in 15 minutes
traipse across
the parking lot
and the railroad tracks
just as the train
honking like a goose
hurtles my way
and am lucky
all I lose is a shoe
on my way to work.

Now in my eighties,
the morning ritual
takes half an hour
as hubby makes
sure I don't trip
over a tarantula
or stumble and fall
and break bones
as I shower and shampoo
and we tussle with tangles
and slipping arms in sleeves.

Where Did They Go?

The fifty something couple
who settled our land.
He was tanned, dark haired
and so strong he built
the clay house with his own
hands, drilled a well
and a septic system.

She – blonde and so young
looking the firemen building
a barbecue pit on the hill
saw her hiking and mistook
her for a teenager. She lifted
20-pound weights, kickboxed,
belly danced and used her body
like a plank of wood.

Together they traveled
in the summer
across three states for family
reunions staying in motels
swimming and soaking
in hot tubs and returned
with grandchildren via
The Grand Canyon, taking
them to caves, amusement
parks, restaurants and movies.

The white-haired couple now
living in the house are worn
out just making the 80 mile
round trip to Wal-Mart every
12 days for groceries that
they take long daytime naps.
\
But what worries me
is that they get so engrossed
in internet movies they leave
pots sizzling on the stove
until they are blackened.
And I fear they may burn
down the house their younger
selves built for them.

The Cards I Carry in my Wallet Show My Hand

In the 1971 Press Pass
signed by the sheriff
of Los Angeles County
I smile – a young blonde
covering crime
for the Daily Signal
in Huntington Park.

With a cockatiel
on my shoulder,
in dark curly hair
and a Colgate smile,
I pose at the wild
animal park
for the Escondido
Times-Advocate
in the 1975 Press Pass.

A brunette in bangs,
I smile in the 1979
ID card issued by
the San Diego Police
when I report news
for the Coast-Dispatch
in Del Mar, Solana
Beach and Encinitas.

My photo is missing
on colorful cards I hand
to clerks in Albertsons,
Safeway and Bashes,
Good Apple, Borders
and Ulta as I purchase
groceries, vitamins, books
and cosmetics in Idaho,
California and Arizona.

There's also no photo
on the Golden Age Passport
which give me a free pass
to Yellowstone Park
and the Grand Canyon,
Medicare insurance
card and my Visa Card.

My headshot appears again
on my 2020 Arizona Driver's
License in white hair
and glasses, I purse red lips
wondering who will expire first -
me or my Driver's License.

In Our Senior Years

You steady me
when I shake,
catch me
when I stumble,
stand outside
the shower,
handing me
soap and shampoo,
serve me smoothies,
soup, salad and sundaes.

I act as your ears
and eyes
when you remove
your hearing aides
and glasses
and go deaf
and blind
and sleep
through the screeching
smoke alarm
and chorusing coyotes.

When you sit up
saying, *Didn't you scream*
my name? I soothe you.
It's just a nightmare,
as your mother did

and you smile
and fall back to sleep
like when you were
a child more than seven
decades ago.

As the Head Turns

I am sky diving
without a parachute,
bungee jumping
without a cord,
spinning on
the roller coaster
that never stops.

Welcome
to Vertigo,
just turn
your head
and you are there.

I Press the Button

I would like to place
an order, I say.

What would you like?
he asks.

Burger smothered
in gravy on a biscuit.

No biscuits. How about
potatoes and peas?

Fine, I say. He says:
Give me a few minutes.

He walks through the door
and plops a plate on the tray

by the bed and we eat dinner
while watching Reba on TV.

I like the new walkie-talkies
he orders after I bounce off

the wall walking across
the house to find him.

Returning from Walgreens Four days Before Christmas

I recognize an old friend
walking her aging lab
along the dirt road,
long lanky legs
striding
like the palominos
she and her husband
used to straddle.

She leans into the window
and says we look the same
as two decades ago. *My*
eighty-one-year old legs
don't work anymore, I say.
Two days ago, I was paralyzed
and couldn't walk, she says.
And I'm only sixty- seven.

We ask about her eighty-four
year-old husband. *He got bit*
by a rattlesnake trying to move
it with tongs, got stuck on the roof
and lost in the desert, The firemen
found him a mile from our house.

She says she's still nursing at the hospital
but she may have to quit. *I want him to stay*
as long as he can in our home. He is happy.

We wish each other Marry Christmas
but I am not feeling the spirit until my friend
who lost both feet from diabetes
and his beautiful blind wife smile
at me from the Christmas card.

The Sixty-Two-Year-old Barber

who has been cutting
my husband's hair
for over a decade is bloated,
hooked to an oxygen tank,

hobbling on a walker,
hands shaking so bad
he almost chops off
my husband's ear.

Two months later,
when his hair curls
around his collar
like a cat, hubby stops

at the barber shop
near the saddle shop
expecting to find a new
barber with bad news.

Instead, he does
a doubletake as he sees
his old barber, face pink
as a pig, body half its size,

whistling as he waltzes
around the chair, whipping
out a cape and scissoring
and shaving with steady hands.

As he cuts and clips,
he tells a tale
about feeling like he
was hit by a freight train,

falling to the floor
in his double-wide
where he lies there
for nine hours

until a neighbor finds him
and calls 911
and he is resurrected
from the dead.

Halleluiah brother, he says
smiling and waving his hands
as he unveils a perfect sculpture
on my husband's white head.

My Sister Who Walks Three Miles A Day

tells me at the age if 78
she can't walk across the floor
or play with her grandsons
without running out of breath.

It takes her six months to see
a cardiologist who fits her
with a monitor. Another two
months to run on a treadmill.

Your heart is beating too fast,
the doctor diagnoses and puts
her on medication, which makes
her dizzy and nauseous.

She makes it to her 79th birthday
and then she emails that she
is having an angiogram
to determine if the arteries

in her heart are blocked.
If so, they will insert stents.
Her 84-year-old husband
has stents in every artery.

But her husband doesn't have
our family medical history.
Our mother almost doesn't wake
up from the anesthetic.

Our father hallucinates after surgery
and thinks he's being held captive
and tries to jump out of a window
on the seventh floor.

I remember lying on an operating
table in the seventies feeling
like I am slipping under warm water
as liquid drips into my veins.

Someone is asking me a question
but I can't speak or move
a muscle. I hear frantic voices
from far away, *We're losing her.*

I don't want to worry my sister
so I say nothing. She warns
me she will be in the hospital
overnight so I don't panic

until 48 hours pass and no word.
She's dead. I know it, I say.
Her husband would tell you, mine says.
The phone rings. *Don't answer it,*

I say. *It's bad news.* He puts it on
speaker and when we hear the voice
of my brother-in-law we expect
she is gone and go numb.

The cardiologist found two blocked
arteries and inserted stents, he says.
She wants to talk to you. Her voice
is strong and she is breathing better.

She says she won't be able to just
hit the walking trail tomorrow.
I have to wear a heart monitor
while I do supervised exercises.

She says she was awake during
some of the procedure but sedated
during the worst part. I don't need
to hear any more. My baby sister is alive.

The Lost Men

A jeep and ATV
roll up in the driveway
and three guys -
all in their seventies
with bodies sturdy
and strong – hop out
and tell my husband;
I hear you have
a leak in your well.
We're here to help.

They find it
and fix it but
won't take
any money.
Instead, they pray
for good days ahead.

A decade earlier,
Brian and John
ate chicken and potato
salad and jitterbugged
in our courtyard
as my husband
and Bobby sang
and played guitar.

Brandon says he's
a Browning from Idaho

and likely a distant cousin
to my husband's late wife.
John says my father-in-law
was his favorite teacher.

This is the first time
we've seen John
since he rode off
on his Harley
in a helmet heading
up Highway 66,
while his wife, Shelly,
hung onto his waist
eight years ago.

We haven't seen Neal
since we were evacuated
from the forest fire six
years ago and ate
fresh banana bread
baked by his wife Barbara
in their home on the other
side of town while the men
reminisced about working
with Bobby at the water
plant years earlier.

Three years ago
we last saw Bobby
when he was seventy-eight
and lying in his bed
in assisted living
as my husband called

his lost cell phone
and heard it ringing
from the closet
and found it
in the bottom
of the hamper
in his pants pocket.

In two months,
Bobby was gone.
As they drive off
we hope it isn't
the last we see
of Neal, John
and Brandon.

White Hair Gets Him Waited on in Walmart

my husband says
which is why he
stopped dyeing
his hair brown
after he quit the band.

Most of the checkout
stands are self-serve,
since I stopped
shopping, he says
as he puts away
the cilantro and avocados.

The clerks are so nice.
They ask me if I need
any help and usually
I let them bag up
and ring up
rather than fumble
with arthritic fingers.

His cart was so full,
today, he says, a clerk
steered him to a station
that handled more
items. *You probably*
remind them of their
Dad or grandpa, I say.
He smiles and nods.

I remember my last
walk through Walmart.
My legs collapsed
and a concerned clerk
helped me to the bench
which was removed
during Covid and never
replaced which is why
I stay home while he shops.

On Netflix, We Watch Walt, the Wyoming Sheriff

and his sidekick Standing Bear
chasing outlaws on horseback
across the Indian Reservation.

I remember living on the Ft. Peck
Reservation in the fifties when
the Brockton Big Horn boys win
the Montana State Basketball trophy.

As Walt crosses state lines,
and arrests a cowboy in Billings,
I remember writing news stories
in the sixties for the Gazette.

When he questions a suspect
on Idaho Falls, I recall running
Gem Book Exchange on Maple
Street in the eighties and nineties.

On Hulu, we watch a game
show contestant singing along
to Tim McGraw's song I Like it
I Love it, our song in the nineties.

My eyes closed, I sway as I sing:
I want some more of it. Long
after the contestant has bowed out
and the screen gone dark,

we still sing, sway and swing
like we did three decades ago
even though our joints creak
and our voices crack.

Even Now I Know What I Know

About the age spots,
chronic fatigue,
diabetes and hepatitis,

I'd still sunbathe
in the sand
without sunscreen

to get the Coppertone
tan in California,
Hawaii and Mexico.

Work seven days
a week, twelve hours
a day to report the news.

Drink Crème de cacao
and Singapore slings
and eat banana splits.

Quit my paying job
and live on my savings
in San Miguel and Toronto.

Because it led me to you
and Arizona where we hydrate
our bodies drinking well water

with the wildlife as it cascades
off the rocks into the pond
and off the ice down our throats.

About the Author

Pushcart Prize and Best of the Net Nominated Poet Sharon Waller Knutson is a retired journalist who lives in Arizona. She has published thirteen poetry books including *My Grandmother Smokes Chesterfields* (Flutter Press 2014,) *What the Clairvoyant Doesn't Say* and *Trials & Tribulations of Sports Bob* (Kelsay Books 2021) and *Survivors, Saints and Sinners* (Cyberwit 2022,) *Kiddos & Mamas Do the Darndest Things* (Cyberwit 2022,) *The Vultures are Circling* (Cyberwit 2023) and *The Leading Ladies in My Life* (Cyberwit 2023) and *My Grandfather is a Cowboy* (Cyberwit 2024.) Her work has also appeared in *Poetry Breakfast, Autumn Sky Poetry Review, Poetry Hunger X, Lothlorien, GAS Poetry, Art and Music, The Rye Whiskey Review, Black Coffee Review, ONE ART, Mad Swirl, The Drabble, Gleam, Muddy River Review, Verse-Virtual, Your Daily Poem, Red Eft Review, Beatnik Cowboy, The Five-Two, Impspired and others.*

www.ingramcontent.com/pod-product-compliance
Lightning Source LLC
LaVergne TN
LVHW091057150826
845673LV00002B/611

* 9 7 8 9 3 6 3 5 4 8 3 9 8 *